BETTER BALANCE

Mental health workbook for black men

DAVID QUINN MONTGOMERY

Editing By: *Trenton Munson*
Cover Image: *David Q. Montgomery*
Cover Design: *Aalia Tabassum*
Formatting: *Accuracy4sure*

Blurb

Real success isn't just having an abundance; it's having balance. Achieving and maintaining balance is essential to living a fulfilling life. However, sustaining optimal mental health by creating a proper balance in our lives can be challenging. The various obstacles that black boys and men face have greatly impacted our ability to achieve this allusive state of being. Thus impeding our ability to fully become the best versions of ourselves. Being a black man from the inner city, I've had to face many of these obstacles firsthand. Working in the mental health field for nearly two decades has also greatly contributed to my understanding of this challenging pursuit for many in our communities. This therapeutic workbook highlights aspects of life and mental health that most commonly plague black and brown men when entering therapy. I've dedicated a good part of my life to helping others through the process of pursuing healing and creating life balance. I remain passionate about doing my part to bridge the gap between the culture and addressing mental health. Consequently, this workbook is a useful tool for those on their own personal journey to create a better balance.

Contents

Introduction

This Mental health workbook was created to serve as a therapeutic tool to assist black males in the pursuit of creating a healthy mental and emotional balance. There has been ongoing stigma and need surrounding mental health in the black/brown community for generations. None have been affected more by this disconnect and need than black men themselves. As the view on mental health continues to progress in the black community, more men are being open to the idea of addressing their mental health needs. However, there is still a long way to go regarding exposure, educating, and creating more effective resources these men can utilize. There are many barriers to this issue, a major one being not having nearly enough therapeutic resources relatable to many black men and their particular needs and experiences. Statistics can clearly highlight the large discrepancy between black mental health providers and those of other ethnic backgrounds. Only about 3% of mental health providers and therapists are black. I will always say any good therapy is better than none. However, representation and relatability matter. This became even more evident when I began working more closely with black men through one-on-one therapy. These men often shared a common theme of why they may have never attempted or stuck with therapy in the past: they didn't want to have to explain their cultural experiences.

There is power in seeking healing, as well as the opportunities to collaborate with someone who can understand you culturally and speak your language in the process. Throughout my work as a therapist, getting the opportunity to be a part of the growth and healing of many individuals of various demographics has been rewarding. However, nothing has been more gratifying than working with black men through their healing journey. As a black man, dealing with many of the same day-to-day challenges and experiences, past and present, has challenged me and made me a better therapist and man. In the process of their healing journey, I was able to learn so much about my brothers collectively and myself. The truth is that so many black men are ready to do the work to grow and heal. Unfortunately, for every black man that gets connected to an effective therapist or therapeutic source, there are countless others either waiting but have yet to be reached. Or they have never been even exposed to the idea or conversation. This workbook was developed as a tangible therapeutic tool and introduction to therapy for those men. Also, as a possible asset or extension to the therapeutic process for those who have been or already connected to therapy. Each section of this workbook represents an aspect of mental health that were the most prevalent and/or common needs while working with black men—consisting of TRAUMA, ANXIETY, DEPRESSION, SELF-CARE, RELATIONSHIPS, FRIENDSHIPS/SOCIAL LIFE, and STRESS. Each section allows me to share some culturally specific views of these aspects of mental health developed throughout working with these men and a bit of my own story and experiences. Each section also allows space to reflect, identify potential struggles, find underutilized tools and solutions to those struggles, and do the work to implement them consistently in your life to promote overall balance and healing.

Instructions

All scale questions are based on a scale of 1-10. For some, 1 is the worst, least frequent, or least impactful; while 10 is the best, most frequent, or most impactful. Some scale questions will be the opposite, so be mindful of this when answering each of these questions. The idea here is simple, brother. Each section will have two modules of questions. The first module is specifically to identify problems or areas of need. In the first module, any answer that falls under a 5 is an area of need. In the second module of questions, answers are specifically to identify solutions. Answers to the questions in the second module should ideally be rated at a 7 or higher. Most questions are two-part questions (solutions and implementation), so be sure to answer both for each.

Module 1

This set of questions is to identify potential problems and areas of need. As we go through our daily routines, we often overlook many surface and underlying issues. Exposure to people, places, and situations that trigger our trauma and drain our emotions. Doing so can lead us to be compromised emotionally, sometimes without even being fully conscious of it. Let's explore and navigate these potential problems with just a few straightforward questions. Keep in mind that answers that fall under a 5 in this module need improvement. Answers closer to 1 need significant improvement. Any category with multiple answers under a 5 or below in Module 1 should be an area of focus. For example, if I have four answers rated at 3 in module 1 under stress, I know stress is an area of need and I need to prioritize.

Module 2

This second set of questions explore accessible solutions that may be underutilized. Therapy isn't always filled with revelations of learning new skills to improve. Many times, it's the guidance to rediscover and emphasize the tools and skills you've already possess that are unique to you and your lifestyle. Often, we aren't fully aware of or underestimate the impact and role of these tools and don't implement them nearly enough. The questions in module 2 are to explore the actions, people, thoughts, and behaviors that at some point helped you specifically to sustain emotional stability. Use these answers as your solutions, and when you begin to journal, be sure to refer to these answers and solutions to implement them consistently into your life and routine. Let's highlight these tools and supports and put them to work, king.

Documentation/journaling

This section is the opportunity to put in the work. Like any other process, addressing our mental health and building a better-rounded lifestyle take work to accomplish. Here is the opportunity to track your implementation of the tools, supports, and behaviors you've rediscovered in the previous questions. Focusing on areas of need is key; allow time a space to highlight your successes and failures while implementing them. Set personal goals, be open about your emotions, identify negative thoughts, and don't forget to speak positively! Journaling and recording are proven and effective ways to build mental clarity and strengthen your emotional well-being. Let's put this to practice, brother, and journal your weekly progress for at least 8-9 weeks. Be open, vulnerable, and consistent on your journey to create a better balance.

Tips

If many of your answers in module 1 are low in a particular category but higher in module 2 for the same category, then it may reveal that these tools and actions may not be as effective as you believe them to be. It may be time to explore new ones. If you have many positive or higher rated answers in module 1 but lower scores in module 2, this could mean that it may not be an obvious area of need currently. However, it may reveal less room for growth or sustainability. The goal is to create a better balance across the board in every major phase of life and mental health. Ideally, reaching a 7 or higher in every module for every category can give us the complete balance we strive for.

-After completing the questions from each section, recognize which ones need the most attention based on where you are currently. Time and lifestyle permitted work and journal on as many sections as possible at once. Ideally, working and journaling a few at a time could be more manageable and beneficial. Initially, focus on the areas and sections that currently have the most need. For example, maybe self-care and anxiety are presently the most glaring needs, with many negative or low scores compared to others. Thus, they need the most attention initially. Then work your way up to the areas that may already be solid to explore additional and now conscious ways for possible improvement and sustainability. After nine weeks of journaling on any category, restart the questions again to view your progress.

Lastly, be honest, brother. The first step to healing and building balance is to be real about where you are. Answer questions as truthfully as possible to allow yourself space to grow in the areas you need to. Let's go!

Trauma

Trauma has impacted almost every life to some level and at some point. Individually, these events or life experiences have and can still affect our emotions, reactions, memories, and behaviors. Based on various factors, trauma can impact our brain function and how we see and experience the world. In addition, The Black community has also had a long history of collective trauma that has spanned over generations ranging from racism, poverty, discrimination, violence, and neglect. One of my favorite rappers, Nas, has a verse on one of his albums, "Kings disease," where he says, "If I could've chose, subsidized housin, sometimes witnessing the foulest things would arouse us. We became numb like pure caine on the tongue, to the pains from economical strains." These lines stood out to me so much because of their validity. It highlights how so many traumatic experiences and struggles become the norm when growing up in tough communities and sometimes even become our entertainment.

It's pretty disturbing when you really think about it, but it's been the reality for so many individuals and still is for many young black men. Even for those who didn't grow up in these environments or didn't have these sorts of experiences. We don't often discuss the generational trauma that has been passed down through generations. It compounds the challenges our culture already faces when dealing with our individual trauma. Black men have and still face many collective sources of trauma in their everyday lives. We see law enforcement take the life of someone who looks like us repeatedly and often without consequence. We witness and endure violence and hopelessness in many of our communities. Or the countless friends or loved ones we have lost or been disconnected from without much counsel to help cope or properly grieve. Black men have utilized many ways to attempt to cope with our individual and collective trauma in order to survive and thrive the best way we know. Many of these, unfortunately, haven't always been the healthiest methods, especially long term. Facing and appropriately dealing with our trauma as men is long overdue. Addressing our individual and collective trauma is the beginning steps to healing ourselves, our families, and our community. It will also allow space to break individual and generational strongholds.

Module 1 Questions:

(1 being significant impact, 10 being no impact)

▌ **1. What past or recent experiences would you consider or possibly consider as being traumatic?**

Scale 1-10, how severe was this trauma for you?

▌ **2. What memories impact your mood or trigger a negative emotion in you?**

Scale 1-10, how severe does it impact your mood or emotions?

■ **3. What sort of things do you see or experience now that bring up these memories?**

Scale 1-10, how severe do these memories impact you in any way?

■ **4. How successful have you been with talking about your trauma or these experiences to anyone?**

Scale 1-10, how impactful or helpful was it? (10 being significant impact, 1 being no impact on this question)

■ **5. What ways do you believe that your trauma impacts your thoughts and behaviors negatively now?**

Scale from 1-10, how severe?

■ **6. Scale 1-10, how difficult is it to talk about your trauma? (1 being very difficult, 10 being no difficulty)**

Module 2 Questions:

▪ **1. Name 3 or more things, actions, and people that can help calm you down or possibly change your mood for the better when faced with a traumatic memory or situation that triggers your trauma?**

Scale: from 1-10, how often do you utilize at least 1 from each category daily? (1 being never, 10 being very frequent)

Scale: which number of these options per day, if used, do you feel would be most helpful to you?

Scale 1-10, how frequently do you use them daily? (1 being never, 10 very frequent)

▪ **2. What gets in the way of you accessing these supports consistently?**

Scale 1-10, how often do these barriers get in the way? (1 being very frequent, 10 being never)

3. Name four things you could do to overcome or minimize these barriers?

Scale 1-10, how often do you take these actions? (1 being never, 10 being very frequent)

4. How often are you exposed to whatever triggers your memories of your trauma?

Scale: 1-10 (1 being very frequent, 10 being never)

5. What actions do you take not to have negative emotions take over you when exposed?

Scale from 1-10, how often do you take these actions, and how successful are they? (1 being never and unsuccessful, 10 being very frequent and very successful)

6. What ways have you addressed or discussed your trauma? Which were helpful, which weren't?

Scale: 1-10, how helpful were they? (Rate each individually 1 being not helpful, 10 being very helpful)

7. What thoughts or behaviors do you want to change that possibly stem from your trauma? What positive thoughts and behaviors would you rather have in place of them?

Scale: 1-10, how often do you have the more positive replacement thoughts and behaviors)? (1 being never, 10 being very frequent)

Documentation/journaling:

Write down daily or weekly for nine weeks what you have done to change your reaction to exposure. What steps have been taken to limit your exposure if needed (More emphasis should be placed on thought processes and techniques used to limit negative mental or physical responses when exposed, over avoidance)? Rate yourself each day or week on how successful overall you were with replacing negative thoughts. Rate yourself on a scale of 1-10 each time. Record progress until you feel you've reached a 7 or higher. Write down daily or weekly how often you shared or discussed your trauma (with a therapist, a loved one, or a friend). Record your mood or feelings after each time on a scale of worst to best. Write down daily or weekly what you have done to change or limit your exposure. Record until you feel like you can discuss trauma with mood not becoming negative consistently. Write down daily or weekly what you have done to better eliminate the barrier. Write down what you did to contribute or have better access to things, actions, or people? Record your progress until you feel it reflects a 7 in your life.

Tools:

Thought tracking:

- ☀ Whenever you have a negative thought, intentionally follow it up and replace it with one of your positive and likely more rational alternative thoughts. (Our thoughts lead to feelings; feelings lead to behaviors. Make sure to incorporate your successes and challenges with this throughout your journaling)

Timeline:

- ☀ Create a brief timeline telling your story.

- ☀ Go from your earliest memories to the present day (year by year)

- ☀ Note the events that stick out in your mind the most, good and bad. (There is power in telling our story and connecting the dots when dealing with our trauma. Often, events we have blocked out our minds or minimized have impacted us more than we realize).

Reflect on your family tree (parents, grandparents, siblings, extended family):

- ❂ Write out names and categorize them by relation to you and your lineage.

- ❂ Explore your family history and behavior patterns within it (Mental health struggles, health issues, substance abuse, etc.) (Oftentimes, rather directly or indirectly, trauma can be introduced or passed down through the family. Reflect on your personal experiences and explore some of the generational trauma within your family that you may have not directly experienced).

Week 1.

Week 2.

Week 3.

Week 4.

Week 5.

Week 6.

Week 7.

Week 8.

Week 9.

Anxiety

"I feel trapped and confused and often dealing with something that's not even there, or thinking or worrying about things that didn't even happen yet. It can feel like being completely uncomfortable or scared in certain large gatherings, especially certain types of crowds. It can be feelings of worry regarding what others are thinking or saying about me. Or some sort of scenario that's running through my mind of something bad that can happen at that moment. This can be magnified in certain environments I am in. I believe that it is a chemical imbalance or the way my brain functions, and it plays a part in me feeling this way at times or as often as I do. Using substances can be helpful to cope with these feelings of fear in moments, but it is not always a healthy option or does me any good long term.

When I began to struggle with these issues, a trigger for me was people thinking I was looking for attention, which was why I often kept it to myself or didn't like to speak out as much about it. I change my mind often regarding major or minor decisions because of feeling unsure, and it makes me question a lot of potential outcomes when I have to make and stay with any choice. This becomes very exhausting. Looking too deep into things and worrying about many different possible outcomes is something I do often as well. I can also easily be swayed, which can feel unsettling. Being a black man, the thoughts and fears that come from a place of possibly "not being able to do" when I'm desperately trying to provide for and protect my family can really weigh on me. Socially, not always having access to Jobs and resources only add to the pressure, anxiousness, and fear that often already exist. The climate and history of this country have greatly contributed to these feelings. Racism, discrimination, poverty, and access have all been prevalent in adding to this battle that I have already struggled with for so long on my own. I desire and try to be a good man and take care of my family. Therefore, breaking laws or causing trouble isn't something in my routine or lifestyle. But even still some moments when I should feel safe, I still don't. For example like, when an officer pulls up behind or beside me when driving home from work. What should feel like safety can often just feel even more like concern or fear."

This was a detailed description of an individual's experience with anxiety and how it affects his life. Anxiety and other mental health struggles can look and feel different to different people. However, many men who struggle with anxiety could possibly relate to some or all of this person's experiences. It is important for us not only to understand and realize our unique individual triggers and stressors with mental health but also our collective and cultural ones.

Module 1 Questions:

■ **1. When do you feel most anxious?**

Scale 1-10, how often does this occur? Scale 1-10, how severe? (1 being very frequent and very severe, 10 being never and no impact)

2. What triggers you to have anxiety?

Scale 1-10, how severe? Scale 1-10, how frequent are you triggered? (1 being very severe and frequent, 10 being no impact and never)

3. What negative feelings occur when you become anxious?

Scale 1-10, how severe? (1 being very severe, 10 being no impact)

4. What behaviors occur that stem from anxiety?

Scale 1-10, how often? How severe? (1 being very often and severe, 10 being never and no impact)

Module 2 Questions:

- 1. **What helps you to deescalate when you feel most anxious? (Name a minimum of three if possible)**

    Scale: 1-10, how often do you implement these daily/weekly in your life? (1 being never, 10 being very frequent)

- 2. **What situations, thoughts, or people trigger your anxiety?**

    Scale 1-10, how often do you encounter them? How much do they impact it? (1 being very frequent and significant impact, 10 being never and no impact. Make sure to give a rating for each that you list)

- 3. **What activities, thoughts, and/or people help decrease your symptoms when you're anxious?**

    Scale 1-10, how often are you engaging in these activities, thoughts, or people? (1 being never, 10 being very frequent)

▓ 4. How often do you force yourself to face what makes you anxious?

Scale 1-10, how successful are you in overcoming your anxiousness in these moments? (1 being never, 10 being very successful)

Documentation/journaling:

Write down daily or weekly for nine weeks what steps you took to implement what helps you to deescalate when you're most anxious. Record what steps you could or did you take to change the result of these encounters. Record what alternative replacement thoughts you can and have used to decrease your anxiety. Record what activities and people you engage in and with that help your anxiety. Record and describe instances you have faced that usually make you anxious, and what actions helped improve your mental and emotional responses in these situations. Record and monitor progress until you feel each category can be marked as a 7 or higher.

Tools:

Create a safety plan (people, places, and actions you can utilize to help you deescalate):

People:

Places:

Actions:

- Incorporate in your recordings how effectively you utilize these when becoming anxious.

Grounding actions (mindfulness):

- Take a short time to be fully present in your body and mind.

- Close your eyes and focus on your breathing.

- Think about how different parts of your body feel as you concentrate on your breathing. Start from your lower extremities and work your way up to each part of your body. You can do this in a quiet relaxing setting or in a busier environment (Headphones could be useful in such an environment.

Earthing:

- Touch and feel objects around you like the ground, grass, trees, or other objects around you if you are indoors. If outdoors and able, place your bare feet on the ground, sit on the grass or concrete, or place some part of your skin on the surface, including your hands. Water on the skin can be helpful as well.

Move and taste:

- ✹ Take a short walk, feel and breathe in some air. Take a drink or food item.

Week 1.

Week 2.

Week 3.

Week 4.

Week 5.

Week 6.

Week 7.

Week 8.

Week 9.

Depression

I fell in love with football at a very young age. I loved everything about it, the competitiveness, the physicality, the comradery, I can go on, but all of it was a joy to be a part of. I felt I could and would play the game forever back then. However, when my playing days ended, I was eventually introduced to my next love, the therapeutic world. As a result, I was away from the game of football for some time; well, at least from up close. This changed when I was blessed with the opportunity to coach at my former high school. I must admit that it felt great to be around the game again, but the opportunity to teach and be around the young men was and is the biggest joy of all. It can also be a major challenge trying to help and guide the lives of many young men outside of the football field. As a coach, the responsibility or skill of keeping players motivated, having them in the right position, or gap or technique was expected in this role.

However, the amount of time and effort it takes to attend to players' personal and emotional needs outside the game is not so much. In just the course of a year during the pandemic, I saw so many young men deal with more disappointment, loss, frustration, and uncertainty than I could imagine. I saw the rigors of the position take their toll emotionally on many of the coaches as well. Some of these challenges include community violence, lack of support and resources, canceled games, etc. Not much of it was due to anything done on the football field at all. And as a result, I also began to witness many physically strong, confident, and lively young black student athletes show up to play, have fun and compete. But once the practices and games ended, I saw many of those same young men isolate, shut down, become angry, uncertain, unmotivated, and hopeless. I saw a lot of depression. The coaches' sincere devotion of love and commitment created a space for them to escape, focus and potentially grow as young men on and off the field. However, we were ill-equipped to address many of the emotional needs of these young people, causing them to just have to move forward despite this need not being met or even discussed. In reality, many of these young men had no idea what they were even dealing with. Thus, numbness began to take over due to the challenges.

The difficulties many young black men face in this country are real and very common in our underserved communities. Many events throughout history have highlighted these issues in our minority communities. The Covid 19 pandemic just did it most effectively for this social media era. What was once again highlighted during this time was revealing, but nothing new. This is just another small example of how this cycle and trend of not recognizing emotional needs can begin very early in life and can often lead into our adulthood. Suffering in silence, not facing and dealing with our emotions, and not getting support. Sitting in sadness, discontent, and pain and just moving along. So many of our brothers in the ladder years of life are still dealing with this same trend that began early. We haven't been given the tools nearly enough to learn how to recognize when depression invades our lives and what we need to come out of it. It is a must to do so, as well as teach our younger generation what is required to continue to break these destructive cycles.

Module 1 Question:

■ **1. When do you feel most withdrawn, unmotivated and/or sad?**

How long does it usually last when it occurs?

Scale from 1-10, how severe are these feelings when they occur? (1 being very severe, 10 being no impact)

Scale 1-10 what are the durations of these feelings typically when they occur? (1 being very long weeks or months, 10 being very brief, maybe hours)

■ **2. What triggers these emotions?**

Scale 1-10, how frequent do you encounter these triggers? (1 being very frequent, 10 being never).

Scale 1-10, how severe is the emotional reaction when you encounter them? (1 being very severe, 10 being no impact)

▓ **3. What are your most common thoughts before you feel these emotions?**

Scale 1-10, how much do these thoughts impact your emotions? (1 being very much, 10 being no impact)

▓ **4. What are your behaviors when you feel these emotions?**

Scale 1-10, how frequent do these behaviors occur? (1 being all the time, 10 being never) Which of these would you like to change?

Module 2 Questions:

▓ **1. What activities, people, and actions help you to prevent or change these emotions or the duration in which they last? (Name three from each category)**

▓ **2. What can you do to uplift yourself or your mood once you are triggered?**

Scale 1-10, how often do you do this daily or weekly? (1 being never, 10 being very often)

3. What positive or more rational thoughts can you put in place of the negative thoughts that lead to negative emotions? (Name one positive for each negative thought that usually occurs)

Scale: 1-10, how often do you do this? (1 being never, 10 being very often)

4. What are some alternative behaviors to the ones that you would like to change when you feel these emotions? (Name two alternative behaviors for each usual behavior).

Scale: 1-10, how often do you use these alternative behaviors? (1 being never, 10 being very often)

Tools:

**Exercise/physical activity:*

- Whether in the gym or on your own, partake in some physical activity or exercise. If in the home, simple pushups, stretches, yoga, and HIIT workouts are very effective forms of exercise, require no equipment, and are available on various platforms such as YouTube.

**Proper sleep:*

- Search and discover natural sleeping aids and create a conducive environment for sleep.

Meditation and music:

- ☀ No need for any awkward poses and tranquil sounds brother if not your speed. Simply put on the favorite tunes of your choice and create a relaxing setting of your liking. Pray, think, breathe, and relax. Add smells to enhance the experience by cooking, using candles, or diffuser oils.

Have fun:

- ☀ Challenge yourself to partake in the activities you enjoy in and out of the home. Don't consistently isolate.

Live more, social media less:

- ☀ Research shows a significant association between depression and high social media usage. Social media has its place and benefits. However, over utilization can negatively impact us more than we realize. Put down the phone, be in the moment more often, and find a healthy balance.

Separate yourself from the condition:

- ☀ Depression is not who you are but something that has invaded your life. Be mindful of the situations, circumstances and behaviors that often invite depression in.

Documentation/journaling:

Write down daily or weekly for nine weeks how often you engage with the activities, people, and actions that prevent or change your depressive emotions. Record how often you are triggered, as well as your successes in uplifting your mood when triggered and how. Record how often you replaced a negative thought with a positive one, and keep track of those thoughts and how they made you feel. Record what alternative behaviors you utilized when triggered. Record and track progress until you feel each category reflects a 7.

Week 1.

Week 2.

Week 3.

Week 4.

Week 5.

Week 6.

Week 7.

Week 8.

Week 9.

Self-care

Proper self-care is something that has plagued our culture for generations. Many of us have developed the mentality that being busy leads to success. We have often put our drive to succeed and provide for ourselves and our loved ones over our natural self-care needs. I've even heard many very successful motivational speakers talk about sacrificing or ignoring proper sleep and rest to reach monetary and/or professional goals. I've experienced many clients who have also functioned in this manner or adopted this mindset as well. Being a part of a race that has endured so much generational poverty, I can concur with the desire and urge firsthand to want to break these cycles. I understand the urgency to financially take care of our loved ones, be financially free, and possibly create wealth. However, I couldn't disagree more with these particular notions of ignoring sleep, rest, etc., to accomplish it than I already do. Yes, time, sleep, and other sacrifices have to be made throughout our lives in moments to achieve our goals, but they should never be at the expense of our overall mental and physical health. We have to begin to change this narrative in our culture of what success looks like. Being financially stable is important. Job titles, social media followers, and professional achievements can be impactful. However, true success lies within those who have created and maintained a healthy balance across all aspects of life, including self-care. By creating this balance and practicing better self-care, we allow space and opportunity to enjoy our accomplishments and all that life has to offer. We give ourselves more opportunities to live in the moment and be present. We create more chances to possibly prologue our lives while creating better mental, spiritual, and emotional clarity, which will only enhance our overall well-being and relationships.

■ **1. What makes you feel overwhelmed?**

Scale 1-10, how severe is it when it occurs? (1 being very severe, 10 being no impact)

■ **2. What situations, people, or places drain you the most?**

Scale 1-10, how severe is this response? (1 being very severe, 10 being no impact).

Scale 1-10, how frequently do you encounter them? (1 being very frequently, 10 being never)

■ **3. Scale 1-10, how often do you feel overwhelmed? (1 being very frequent, 10 being never)**

▌ 4. Scale 1-10, how often do you feel sleep deprived or exhausted? (1 being very   frequent, 10 being never)

▌ 5. Scale 1-10, how do you feel about your overall physical health and diet? (1 being terrible, 10 being excellent)

▌ 6. Scale 1-10, how content are you with your weekly routine and schedule when considering downtime and rest? (1 being very unsatisfied, 10 being very content)

Module 2 Questions:

▌ 1. What are the activities that relax you the most? (name at least three you can do on your own and three that involve others)

Scale 1-10, how often do you partake in these activities daily/weekly? (1 being never, 10 being very frequent)

■ **2. What activities or actions help you to transition into getting rest?**

Scale 1-10, how often do you partake in these activities daily/weekly? (1 being never, 10 being very frequent)

Scale 1-10, how often do you get 6-8 hours of sleep/rest daily in a week? (1 being never, 10 being very frequent)

■ **3. What physical activities do you most enjoy for exercise?**

Scale 1-10, how often do you partake in these activities daily/weekly? (1 being never, 10 being very frequent). What foods/products do you feel are a good fit for your lifestyle to promote healthy eating and intake (make a list of 5-10 food items)?

Scale 1-10, how often do you eat these foods/items daily/weekly? (1 being never, 10 being very frequent)

■ 4. What hobbies and/or enjoyable activities do you engage in or would like to?

Scale 1-10, how often do you engage in these daily/weekly? (1 being never, 10 being very frequent)

Documentation/journaling:

Write down daily or weekly for nine weeks how often you engage in the activities that help relax you (involving at least two from each list). Record how effectively you are transitioning into rest as well your progress in pursuing 6-8 hours of rest per day. Include what things impede or improve your progress and how you can adjust each. Record your exercise frequency based on your needs. Record your successes in incorporating your food items and products, and record barriers. Record what hobbies and enjoyable activities you have been able to engage in weekly. Record the challenges and how you felt after. Record and track progress until you feel each category reflects a 7.

Tools:

Plan ahead:

* Map out your week before the week starts. Write down an ideal schedule for the week with a balance of normal responsibilities (kids, work, errands, etc.) and self-care activities (fitness, hobbies, intimacy, reading, activities from question 1).

One for One practice:

- ❂ Add at least one self-care activity for every responsibility each day. Keep in mind IMPLEMENTATION over DURATION. Even if you're only able to do a self-care activity for a short duration due to your schedule, make sure you do it. For example, if you like to read or catch your favorite podcast for two hours after work before bed and the day only allows time for 30 minutes, read or listen for 30 minutes.

Check yourself:

- ❂ When actively practicing self-care, ask yourself these three questions before engaging in anything outside of it.
    1. Is it my problem?
    2. Do I have to respond/address it?
    3. Do I have to respond/address it right now?

Money management:

- ❂ Overworking ourselves and ignoring self-care isn't always out of necessity. Bad money management often plays a huge role in this issue. Set a budget, educate yourself financially with research, use financial advisors, and most importantly, address your mental health. How we manage money greatly affects our mental and emotional health.

Always make a deposit

- ❂ Consider yourself the most important account you'll ever have; make sure to make a deposit each day.

Week 1.

Week 2.

Week 3.

Week 4.

Week 5.

Week 6.

Week 7.

Week 8.

Week 9.

Friendships/Social Life

Growing up in the inner city, one thing that has always seemed to matter for many young men, or something they took pride in one way or another, is where they were from. What neighborhood or block you lived or grew up in has long been a sense of identity for many young black men. In many cases, it has led to gangs and other negative affiliations. However, in many other cases, it was just a form of belonging to something, such as a group or even an area for many young men. As humans, we often all have that innate desire to want to belong and be a part of something. As men, that desire in us runs even deeper. It is displayed in my earlier example about competitive team sports or just the group of homies that you called your brothers. Comradery matters a lot to boys and, therefore, men and has become a part of our psychological makeup as much as anything else. With the challenges black men have faced in this country and around the world, the community, your block, and your brothers can give a sense of strength and purpose. For so long, black men have been put in a position or the mindset to be strong, endure, and stand on their two alone. We need to have that ability. However, being able to maintain a solid circle is essential as well. Support, accountability, collaboration, or simply being able to be one of the guys at times is often more imperative to men's functioning and mental than we give credit for. Many species thrive when they belong to a pack, however large or small. Men are no exception to this evolutionary rule and also thrive when they're a part of the right pack. Social life and friendships matter for men's mental health. Effectively navigating through this aspect of our lives can promote growth and lasting mental stability.

■ **1. Scale 1-10, how often do you feel isolated or lonely? (1 being very often, 10 being never)**

What situations lead to isolation? After what duration of little to no meaningful connections do you typically begin to feel lonely?

Scale 1-10, how frequent does this occur? (1 being very often, 10 being never).

■ **2. Scale 1-10, how confident do you feel in your ability to rely on at least three people (2 non-family) in your life for help or to talk to? (1 being not at all, 10 being very confident)**

■ **3. How do you typically feel when you engage your friends and/or loved ones?**

Scale 1-10, if positive, how frequently do you engage them? (1 being never, 10 being very often).

■ 4. How do you feel when you attend social events that you enjoy?

Scale 1-10, if positive, how often do you attend? (1 being never, 10 being very often).

Module 2 Questions:

■ 1. Name everyone (at least three or more, if unable to list three, rate below 5 on the scale) you feel you can reach out to when you need support or begin to feel isolated?

Scale 1-10, how often do you reach out or engage these individuals when you begin to feel this way? (1 being never, 10 being very frequent)

■ 2. Name every one you can reach out to for help or talk to (at least three, rate under a 5 if unable to).

Scale 1-10, how often do you reach out to these individuals when this occurs? (1 being never, 10 being very frequent)

■ **3. If engaging your friends to bring out positive emotions and experiences, scale 1-10, how often do you engage your friends (balance your answer based on in-person and phone contact)? (1 being never, 10 being very often)**

■ **4. If you prefer social events to bring out positive emotions and experiences, scale 1-10, how often do you partake? (1 being never, 10 being very frequent)**

Documentation/Journaling:

Record daily/weekly for nine weeks how frequently you engage someone on your list before and after a feeling of isolation or loneliness. Record successes, regression, and barriers. Record how often you reach out to or engage individuals on your list when desired. Record how, what interactions, and with whom. How often are these interactions? Record how often you are engaging socially. What social events and/or activities have you enjoyed, and which not so much? Monitor how frequent these occur and how healthy and beneficial they feel to you. Record progress until you feel it reflects 7 or above.

Tools:

Plan ahead:

- ☀ Plan social outings or get together with friends at least once a month. Setting dates allow people to plan around their busy schedules. (Don't hesitate to do things on your own when necessary, solo outings can be gratifying).

Be accessible:

- We all have busy lives, but being accessible is important to maintaining solid friendships. You may not always attend or be present physically, but periodic and consistent calls and texts can go a long way to maintaining solid friendships.

Step outside the box:

- Brother, don't hesitate to have different experiences with your friends outside the norm. Don't get it twisted; we've all had our fair share of local club and bar outings. But don't wait to travel and see new places with your circle. Create new experiences with your friends, plan road trips, and try different activities outside the norm to build and maintain those lifelong bonds.

Week 1.

Week 2.

Week 3.

Week 4.

Week 5.

Week 6.

Week 7.

Week 8.

Week 9.

RELATIONSHIPS

I've been asked on many occasions, "What made me become a therapist, or what drew me to therapy." I often don't have a clear answer because it's something I never planned or thought about growing up. Sports, particularly football, was always my passion. Therefore, when it comes to the world of therapy, it was something that God chose for me to be in, which I grew a love and passion for. I enjoy many aspects of it, and some not so much, to be totally transparent. Many aspects of the work ignite my energy and intrigue my curiosities. Being a part of the healing process for those I get to work with, as well as attempting to contribute to the change in how therapy is viewed in my culture, are the main motivations for me.

With that said, when I think about it in-depth, the one aspect that intrigues me the most is relationships. To me, it's the most important part of the work, and maybe life. Relationships in some way, shape, or form should always come into play during therapy. It should be when working with couples or families but even working with individuals as well, regardless of the presenting issues. Relationships, whether intimate, kinship or others, influence men's lives, functioning, and mental health. I would say that 100% of the men I have worked with have been dealing with some sort of dysfunction or discontent with one or various relationships in their lives. It's something we all deal with and experience. However, for many black men, it's not something we have always been able to navigate through successfully. I believe that to be the case due to various factors. A few being trauma, recognizing and dealing with our emotions, effective communication, lack of vulnerability, and lack of effective and sustained boundaries. These have greatly impacted our ability to build and maintain healthy relationships. By never learning or addressing many of these issues or skills, many of our brothers have gone through lifetimes of struggling relationships. Recognizing how our past and present relationships impact our mental health and well-being is essential. Also, identifying how we may contribute to these relationships' struggles can be life-changing. Relationships can be infinite and complex, naturally simple or forcefully complicated. A key to optimizing this part of our lives is the understanding that experiences always go beyond just our own. On the other side of it, there will always be another experience, perspective, and interpretation. Understanding and accounting for this element will bring us clarity and allow us to protect ourselves while also allowing space to grow where needed.

Module 1 Questions:

- 1. Scale 1-10, how often have you felt negative emotions based on or caused by your intimate relationship(s) or dating life past or present? (1 being very frequent, 10 being never)

- 2. Describe your overall relationships in one word (one word each to describe each separate set of relationships... family, friends, intimate).

Scale 1-10, how would you rate the overall quality of these relationships (rate each separately 1 being very low quality, 10 being very high quality)

3. Which relationships in your life more often bring out positive emotions or interactions?

Scale 1-10, how frequently do you engage in these relationships? (1 being never, 10 being very frequent)

4. Which relationships more often bring out negative emotions or interactions?

Scale 1-10, how frequently do you engage these people and/or relationships? (1 being very often, 10 being never)

5. If question number 2 was asked to some of the individuals in each category, what do you believe their one-word description of their relationship with you would be, and Why?

Scale 1-10, what ratings would you predict to receive from each set of people: family, friends/associates, and intimate, regarding the quality of their relationship with you? (1 being very low quality, 10 being the best)

🔹 6. Describe what negative emotions seem to be present or come up most often regarding your intimate relationships.

Who or what triggers these emotions?

🔹 7. How do you usually react?

Scale 1-10, how helpful do you believe those reactions are to the relationship or your feelings? (1 being not helpful at all, 10 being very helpful)

🔹 8. What traits or behaviors do you exhibit that prevent you from getting your needs met in relationships?

Scale 1-10, how frequently do they get in the way? (1 being very often, 10 being never)

🔹 9. What traits or behaviors do you exhibit that prevent you from meeting others' needs in relationships?

Scale 1-10, how frequently do they get in the way? (1 being very often, 10 being never)

Module 2 Questions:

- **1. What reactions do you feel would be or have been more helpful when these negative emotions or triggers occur?**

Scale 1-10, how often do you implement these reactions? (1 being never, 10 being very frequent)

- **2. How often do you engage the individuals who more often bring out positive emotions on**

a scale of 1-10? (1 being never, 10 being very frequent)

- **3. For individuals you listed, who more often bring out negative emotions, how often do you implement your more "helpful" reactions when engaging or triggered by them, scale 1-10? (1 being never, 10 being very frequent)**

- **4. What traits or behaviors do you exhibit that may bring out negative emotions or reactions in the people in each of the three relationship categories?**

Scale 1-10, how would you rate your mindfulness of these traits and/or behaviors when engaging these individuals? (1 being never, 10 being very frequent?

5. What traits or behaviors do you exhibit that usually bring out positive emotions in each of these three relationship categories?

Scale 1-10, how would you rate your mindfulness of these traits and/or behaviors when engaging these individuals? (1 being never, 10 being very frequent)

6. What traits or behaviors do you exhibit that most often help successfully build closeness with others?

Scale 1-10, how frequently do you exhibit these behaviors and traits when engaging in relationships? (1 being never, 10 being very often)

7. What traits or behaviors do you exhibit that best assist you in getting your needs met by others' in your relationships?

Scale 1-10, how frequently do you exhibit these behaviors and traits when engaging in relationships? (1 being never, 10 being very frequent)

■ 8. What traits or behaviors do you exhibit that best assist you in meeting others' needs in your relationships?

Scale 1-10, how frequently do you exhibit these behaviors and traits when engaging in your relationships? (1 being never, 10 being very frequent)

Documentation/Journaling:

Record daily/weekly for nine weeks how often you are able to express these negative emotions that occur when triggered by your partner or family member. Record outcomes and/or feelings after these interactions? Were they helpful or not? What seems to be the barriers when not helpful? Record progress until your outcomes or reactions reflect a 7 or higher. Record daily/weekly how frequently you are getting to engage the individuals who bring more positive emotions based on your lifestyle. Record progress and/or regression of frequency of these interactions until you feel the consistency reflects a 7 or higher. When engaged with individuals who trigger negative feelings or emotions, record how often you implement your more "helpful" reactions or behaviors. Record progress and/or regression until you feel it reflects a 7 or higher. Be mindful of barriers that prevent progress. Talk to the individual(s) in each category about traits or behaviors you display that trigger negative emotions in them. Record how mindful you are of displaying these traits when engaging them. Record progress, regression and/or barriers until it reflects a 7 or higher.

Tools:

Set boundaries:

- Set roles and expectations for people in your life based on what they have presented to you throughout your relationship. Allow levels of access to yourself (space, time, and energy) based on those set roles and expectations for each individual. (Most of us have struggled with developing proper skills for creating and maintaining healthy boundaries with others especially loved ones and intimate relationships. Strengthening this is essential in helping improve our relationships overall).

- Set boundaries with yourself and stick to them! (Know your strengths and weakness, and set boundaries with yourself to be able to control what you can when it comes to others).

Develop and improve emotional intelligence:

- Become more aware of your own emotions and feelings so you can better connect and empathize with others' emotions and feelings.
- Practice reflecting on different emotions and feelings you experience throughout the day and why, put a name to them).

Listen more and observe more:

- Having the gift of gab is cool and all king, but we can significantly improve our ability to empathize and better connect with people in our lives by listening more and observing more intently. We can connect better with the feelings and emotions of our loved ones by simply being more observant and better active listeners. It will allow more space to appropriately respond to these feelings and emotions. This will help us to better recognize others' experiences of us directly, as well as better understand and connect with the people we share these relationships with.

***Reflect and Ask questions:**

- Explore your close personal connections and distant ones with family members and note reasons. Also, explore family members' close and/or distant connections with each other.

- Reflect on your family upbringing and relationships within it growing up. Learn more about your family and history by asking elders if possible. Explore how or if some of these patterns could possibly be impacting you currently. (Often, how we function in relationships stems from where relationships began for us, which is family).

***Know your worth King:**

- In many relationships, we can often put others' wants and needs before our own. It's important to be intentional about upholding your end of the bargain in a reciprocal relationship. But understand the value you bring to your relationships, and don't hesitate to hold others accountable to reciprocate when needed.

***Refocus**

- Focus more on the person and the dynamic of the relationship than the structure of it. We too often create anxieties and discontentment trying to conduct ourselves in conjunction with labels, titles, and relations. Instead, put more focus on the reality of the actual interaction and approach accordingly.

Connection vs. compatibility

- ✦ Because you connect doesn't mean you're compatible; because you are compatible doesn't mean you connect. We all have people that we are just naturally and innately drawn and connected to, even if we can't get on the same page. While others may fit easily in our world and mindset, something often indescribable just isn't there or missing. Having both, of course, is ideal. However, true connections are so rare. If present, attempt to build and negotiate ways to improve compatibility. Compatibility can look and feel great from the start, but a lack of connection will always surface if not built and done so organically.

Week 1.

Week 2.

Week 3.

Week 4.

Week 5.

Week 6.

Week 7.

Week 8.

Week 9.

STRESS

Being a therapist is a forever evolving profession. That's by requirement as well as indirectly through the clients and people you get to work with. Once in the field, regardless of how seasoned a therapist you are, there seems to always be a training, certificate or guideline to complete to continue to provide services and to learn. I've been through my fair share of developmental presentations and training. As in any profession, such requirements can sometimes feel repetitive and mundane, other times informative. However, one in particular that I'd never forgotten and that grabbed my attention was a presentation about stress that I attended shortly after grad school. We all know what stress is and what it can do. But taking a deeper look into its overall impact was intriguing and terrifying at the same time. Stress affects us all, and much of how society functions, in general, elicits more of it to enter our lives. For many black men, patterns of stressful behaviors and thinking can be like a parasite passed down to us from birth. As we move forward in life, our thoughts, relationships, desires, obstacles, and experiences can feed this mental and emotional parasite until it literally devours us from the inside out. It will not only beat up our minds but also our bodies. Stress is literally a killer in our community and one of the biggest hurdles for us to learn how to manage. Every aspect of life mentioned in this workbook can feed or limit the stress we encounter.

Managing stress is probably the number one and most frequent goal of the men I have worked with through therapy. So much of our existence has been intertwined with stress and functioning under it instead of learning ways to manage it or even eliminate it. We have ignored its effects for far too long out of a sense of ignorance or obligation to always keep going and be strong, and it's literally killing us. Being a Black man, especially in America, has taught us how to live and function under significant stress and trauma from a very young age. Often, this occurs circumstantially and environmentally even before we ever get to encounter our own individual stressors. As a culture, it's become so much a part of functioning, with few resources and options to actively learn how to manage it effectively. Throughout my life and my work, one of the things that has hurt or angered me the most is seeing young black boys living under constant traumatic stress. Stress has become a normal part of life for them, where it's often not even recognized or acknowledged but the impact is always substantial whether seen or unseen.

Module 1 Questions:

- **1. On a scale of 1-10, how often do you feel stressed or overwhelmed? (1 being very often, 10 being never).**

On a scale of 1-10, how would you rate your overall stress level at least 50% of the time? (1 being very high, 10 being little to no stress)

▪ **2. What activities, people, or responsibilities trigger feelings of stress the most?**

    Scale 1-10, how severe are these feelings when they occur (rate each individually, 1 being very severe, 10 being very minor)

▪ **3. What thoughts are often present or become prevalent when you feel stressed?**

    Scale 1-10, how often do these thoughts occur? (1 being very often, 10 being never)

▪ **4. What thoughts trigger feeling stress?**

    Scale 1-10, how often do these thoughts occur? (1 being very often, 10 being never)

▪ **5. How does your body feel when stressed?**

    Scale 1-10, how severe are these feelings? (1 being very severe, 10 being very minor)

▪ 6. Scale 1-10, how often do these feelings in your body occur? (1 being very often, 10 being never)

Module 2 Questions:

▪ 1. What activities and people help keep down your stress levels?

Rate how often you engage in these activities or utilize these people on a scale of 1-10? (1 being never, 10 being very often)

▪ 2. What thoughts occur that add to or trigger your stress? What are some alternative thoughts that you can have to combat or lower stress levels in these moments?

Rate how often you practice this on a scale of 1-10. (1 being never, 10 being very often)

▪ 3. What activities or people help bring down stress levels when stressful events or circumstances occur?

Scale 1-10 when stressed, rate how often you engage in these activities or supports. (Rate separately, 1 being never, 10 being very often)

■ 4. What behaviors or actions can you implement to defeat or prevent stress consistently?

Scale 1-10, how often do you implement these? (Rate separately, 1 being never, 10 being very often)

Documentation/Journaling:

Record daily/weekly for nine weeks the activities and interactions that seem to contribute to maintaining healthy stress levels for you throughout the week. Rate your success and overall frequency of these engagements at the end of the week on a scale of 1-10. Record the frequency of stressful thoughts that occurred throughout the week. Record each time you were able to replace these initial thoughts. Rate your overall success with this each week on a scale of 1-10. If stressful events have occurred or are present, record what activities or relationships you engaged in that help balance your stress level. On a scale of 1-10, how successful were you each week in engaging in or with these? Continue to record progress until you feel each reflects a 7 or higher weekly.

Tools:

Plan Ahead:

- The most effective way to combat stress is to get ahead of it by engaging in consistent self-care behaviors and utilizing the activities, people, and thoughts that are helpful before stressful events even occur.

Practice better time management

- Know when and how to say no. Create a balance in your schedule.

Control what you can control, brother:

- *There is so much stress due to circumstantial and environmental factors often out of our control. Focusing on what we can control in these moments (thoughts, activities, and relationships) is essential in our ability to manage our stress.

Meditation and prayer:

- Spirituality can decrease stress by helping us create a sense of stillness and peace. It encourages a better connection with ourselves, others, and God by surrendering stress-inducing worries and troubles to a higher power.

Get moving:

- Incorporate physical activity into your weekly routine; any form of exercise is an effective stress reliever.

Week 1.

Week 2.

Week 3.

Week 4.

Week 5.

Week 6.

Week 7.

Week 8.

Week 9.

The seed that fell among thorns stands for those
who hear, but as they go on their way they are
choked by life's worries, riches and pleasures, and
they do not mature.

But the seed on good soil stands for those with a
noble and good heart, who hear the word, retain
it, and by persevering produce a crop.

Luke 8:14-15

ABOUT THE AUTHOR

David Quinn Montgomery is a clinical therapist out of Philadelphia. He received BA in clinical psychology from West Chester University and a Master's in family & marital therapy from Chestnut Hill College. David has over sixteen years of experience in the mental health field, including working with individuals (children, adolescents, and adults), couples and families. As a former athlete from Inner City Philadelphia, David eventually refocused his interest and passion on mental health due to the glaring need in the community and culture. After working in various communities and demographics, realizing the alarming number of childhood friends and neighbors that were lost or jailed was eye-opening. Helping address many of the issues that plague black and brown men from these communities and all walks of life has become an ongoing passion.

Contact Author: Instagram david_quinn

Facebook.com/David Quinn Montgomery

Quinndavid4459@gmail.com